F ___

Pastor Reginald D. Jordan
Inspiring Temple of Praise Church

And they overcame him by the blood of the lamb, and by the word of their testimony; and they loved not their lives unto death.
Revelation 12:11

With the assent of televangelism, Word conferences, and seminars, the body of Christ has seen an overwhelming display of flesh—men and women— who have perfected the art of inciting flesh. This truth forces us to admit that there are very few who attend these conferences and seminars who come away having had a real experience with the power of God. Nevertheless, the Lord has always had a secret weapon when it involves the liberating of souls from the bondage of sin—a **Word of Testimony**.

Elder Patricia Miller has endeavored to reach out to tormented souls and literally snatch them out of the hands of the devil by sharing intimate details about her walk with the Lord. This type of exposure requires much prayer and supplication because it *places on the line everything people think they understand about you. She reaches back and pulls the cover off of past mistakes and victories and unashamedly shares with the reader the details of how the Lord brought her through. This not only takes courage, but also the confidence of knowing that when all is said and done, the Lord will protect the integrity of the ministry and not allow the enemy to make a mockery of what has been shared. Having said this, I rebuke and curse every assignment of the enemy that would attempt to take this literary work out of context and speak life over every soul that would endeavor to read it.*

NO PAIN, NO GAIN *comes from the heart of an individual who understands the importance of sharing her testimony—not for the purpose of glamorizing oneself, but for the sole purpose of glorifying the Lord God Almighty. For in glorifying Him through becoming naked and not ashamed, I am convinced that struggling saints can see a way of escape.*

If you, as the reader, come away from this book with anything, it is quite evident that you will come away with knowing that you, too, can overcome the pain, and press on to the crown that you are intended to gain.

INTRODUCTION

This book is written from my life experiences. I have tried to share with you my personal pains, trials, and a few situations that I have faced. My personal pain is not written to offend anyone who may read this book. When I began writing four years ago, I did not know, then, that I was a writer. I have a friend to whom I used to write letters all the time and she would tell me, then, that I was writing her a book.

This book is written to many that may be struggling with relationships and a call on your life from God for ministry. My prayer is that you will be ministered to through my life story and that you may find some strength, courage, and motivation to run the race that is set before you.

Yours In Christ,
Pat

TABLE OF CONTENTS

DEDICATION
ACKNOWLEDGMENT

ABOUT THE AUTHOR

Printed in the United States of America

Great Impressions
Printing & Graphics
Vickie Lynn Goble
444 West Mockingbird
Dallas, Texas   75247
PH: (214) 631-2665
FAX: (214) 631-4329

ISBN # 0-9702800-0-9

Published by
Eleanor Pat Miller
Destined To Win Ministry

DEDICATION

This book is dedicated to the memory of my mother, Ruth A. Perkins, who went home to be with the Lord on February 21, 2000 at the age of 87 years old and to the memory of my sister, Hattie LaVern Wesley, who also went home to be with the Lord on December 19, 1996 at the age of 48 years old.

I dedicate this book also to my family who endured the changes God was making in my life. To my husband, Don, for twenty-three years of marriage; my son, Jimmy, and my daughter, Erica.

To my sister, Ruthie, who has always been there to fill in for my mother. To my brothers, Thomas and Roy, may this book encourage you in your walk of life.

I pray that if I should leave this earth before you, this will be something that you can share with others—family and friends. God is no respecter of person!

********Special dedication to Bishop T.D. Jakes, Author of **Maximize the Moment.** I do not know you personally, but I want others to know how you affected my life in finishing this book. During the last two months of my mother's life, your book *encouraged me to look ahead. My sister, Ruthie, and I alternated as "Caretaker" for our mom. Every weekend, I stayed with my mother to let my sister go home.*

Bishop, even if you never get a chance to read this book, I want the world to know that I thank God for your sharing your personal time with your mother during her last days. Your book took me through some of the touchiest moments I had to face. Everything I experienced on the weekend with my mother was right there on the next page.

May you and your family continue to be a blessing to the Body of Christ!

ACKNOWLEDGMENTS

To the wonderful people that God allowed to cross my path:

EDITORS

Shirley Lucia	Coworker
Jody Thomas	Coworker
Rev. Reginald Jordan	Pastor, ITOP Church
Sharon A. Burkley	ITOP Church

INTERCESSORS

Missionary Shirley Laws
Minister Linda Gentry
Minister Michelle Osorio
Peggy Johnson

*******Special Thanks to Ruth Mayfield, Author, for sharing her resources, wisdom, and knowledge.

To many other friends, co-laborers in the ministries, other coworkers, and any enemies. It took a mixture of people to encourage me to keep praying, believing, and walking by faith no matter what the cost.

Many thanks to Vickie Goble of **Great Impressions Printing & Graphics** for a job well done.

Chapter One
GOD IS MORE THAN ENOUGH!

El Shaddai

*T*ruly God has saved many of us from darkness to the marvelous light. Let's just stop right now and give Him praise! I can say to you that God is a good God! He is no respecter of person. What He has done for me, He will do for you. What did He do for me? First, He saved me from the pits of Hell. Then, He filled me with His precious Holy Ghost and gave me joy unspeakable and full of glory. When I thought my life was ending, it was actually just beginning.

1

God Is More Than Enough

I started to experience many of life's dilemmas and disappointments including a broken marriage, becoming a single parent, losing my job, financial crises, and broken relationships with so called friends. When I was on the verge of losing my freedom, I thought suicide was the only way out. Oh, but I am so glad to share with you today that I am a survivor. I did not give up. How? Only through the prayers of the righteous.

During most of my trying times, I was not born again nor was I filled with the Holy Ghost. There is a favorite song of mine titled *Somebody Prayed For Me*. I thank God that there is power in prayer! I must be truthful with you; not everything that I suffered was because of Jesus. Sometimes I suffered because **I** made the wrong choices and took the wrong road.

NO PAIN, NO GAIN

When you do not pray or seek God's word you are subject to do anything and go anywhere. Praise God for His omnipresence (being everywhere), for His omniscience (all knowing), and for His omnipotence (all powerful). Today there are many individuals whose lives are like mine. You are trapped within yourself and do not know what to do or how to come out. Just take a look at me; I am a testimony. IT CAN BE DONE!

We are growing every day in His grace. Joy can begin to flow like rivers of living waters. The season is just right. This brings me to another point in my life.

God Is More Than Enough

When I needed peace, the Bible told me this:

> **These things I have spoken unto you, that in me ye might have peace. In the world ye shall have tribulation: but be of good cheer; I have overcome the world.**
>
> *John 16:33*

No one wants to experience pain, but in this life pain is a part of deliverance. That might make you feel like what is the use? The use is that God is not through with you yet. So, don't give up! You are destined to win. Just that statement (destined to win) alone has kept the fire burning on the altar of my heart for others to be set free from the hand of the enemy. God was so merciful to me. He allowed three faith women to receive the vision of my heart---Linda, Penola, and Alice.

NO PAIN, NO GAIN

The vision that I have is based on these words can be seen in Ephesians:

> *And he gave some, apostles; and some, prophets; and some, evangelists; and some pastors and teachers; For the perfecting of the saints, for the work of the ministry, for the edifying of the body of Christ: Till we all come in the unity of the faith, and of the knowledge of the Son of God, unto a perfect man, unto the measure of the stature of the fullness of Christ: That we henceforth be no more children, tossed to and fro, and carried about with every wind of doctrine, by the sleight of men, and cunning craftiness, whereby they lie in wait to deceive.*
> *Ephesians 4:11-14*

God Is More Than Enough

Paul wrote to his son in the ministry, Timothy, *Let the woman learn in silence with all subjection. But I suffer not a woman to teach, nor to usurp authority over the man, but in silence. (I Timothy 2:11-12)*

Paul also wrote this in the book of Galatians:

> *But the scripture hath concluded all under sin, that the promise by faith of Jesus Christ might be given to them that believe. But before faith came, we were kept under the law, shut up unto the faith which should afterwards be revealed. Wherefore the law was our schoolmaster to bring us unto Christ, that we might be justified by faith. But after it is come, we are no longer under a schoolmaster. For ye are all the children of God by faith in Christ Jesus.*

> *For as many of you as have been baptized into Christ have put on Christ. There is neither Jew nor Greek, there is neither bond nor free, there is neither male nor female: for ye are all one in Christ Jesus.*
>
> *Galatians 3:22-28*

After studying these books, I knew that we had been in darkness and we needed freedom. These women sacrificed ten years of their life to work with me in building up other men and women, as well as ourselves, through retreats, conferences, seminars, and traveling to many places to receive the Word of God.

I must also share with you concerning my life in the Spirit with your family. As I write, I have been married for twenty-two years. You may want to ask,

God is More Than Enough

"Is my marriage where I want it to be?" The answer is **NO!** Will it ever be? The answer is **YES!** God said in His word, ***Delight thyself also in the Lord; and He shall give thee the desires of thine heart Commit thy way unto the Lord; trust also in Him; and He shall bring it to pass. (Psalm 37:4-5)***

It is only right for me to be honest. Too many preachers are afraid to tell the truth. Your greatest battle will be with your husband or wife, if you are married, because the enemy does not want to see you and your mate as one.

Why? Because of the anointing. One of my greatest sorrows is to see Christian couples living double lives. They are one way at home and another way at church.   It is time to be real.   We need to let the Holy Ghost guide our marriages.

I am thankful that my husband is a Christian. He is very active in his church and that is another hurdle one may have to cross—being at different locations and eating different food.   Many people can cook the same food, but in many different ways. Everybody likes different meals.   Some eat more and some eat less.   Some like it hot and some like it cold. Some use different kinds of seasonings.

Some people may say that I should be thankful that my husband is a church man.   Please don't get me wrong.   I am very thankful.   But that does not stop me from wanting a Holy Ghost fired up marriage.   I want the love of Jesus pouring out in all of our lives 24/7. Can that be possible? **YES!** I believe the Word— *NOW faith is the substance of things hoped for, the evidence of things not seen. (Hebrews 11:1)*

Whenever I minister to someone wounded, broken, or disheartened, I also minister to myself. I praise God for my daughter, Erica. She is such a blessing to me. Sometimes I forget that she is my child. We are able to communicate all the time. She is my inspiration and physical leaning post in the natural; I thank God for her.

NO PAIN, NO GAIN

When I become spiritually low, she always reminds me of what I have said to someone else over the telephone. This is a very good point for all of us. You must practice what you preach. The world is confused about our faith. We can believe God for healing, jobs, cars, houses, clothes, money, and a mate. But when it comes to staying married, God becomes "less than enough." Marriage is a faith walk.

For we walk by faith, not by sight.
(II Corinthians 5:7)

If we can remain focused, give God time to work on us, and allow our minds to be renewed, then we will have the key to a successful relationship. **It is called time!!!** Do you have the time to wait? **YES!** The Spirit says, Trust in the Lord with all your heart

11

and lean not unto your own understanding. Let Him direct your paths. (Proverbs 3:5-6) We will never know how much we love God until we are willing to suffer for Him. If it were not for the tests, where would we be today? Would we be in our local newspaper under the divorce column or do we want our names recorded in the record book of God that we did not quit?

BE ENCOURAGED!

NO PAIN, NO GAIN

You can make it even if you are married to an unsaved man or woman. He or she can be saved just like the Word says,

> *And if a woman who has a husband who does not believe if he is willing to live with her, let her not divorce him. For the unbelieving husband is sanctified by the wife, and the unbelieving wife is sanctified by the husband; otherwise your children would be unclean, but now they are holy. But if the unbeliever departs, let him depart: a brother or a sister is not under bondage in such cases. But God has called us to peace. For how do you know, O wife, whether you will save your husband? Or how do you know, O husband, whether you will save your wife? (I Corinthians 7:13-18)*

God Is More Than Enough

I remember once when I was teaching Sunday School that one Sunday morning one of my students came in trying to go through the motions. When class was over, she informed some of us that she was leaving church to leave her husband. He was unsaved, on drugs, and everything was a mess. Now, does that sound like anyone you know?

I praise God for surrounding her with sisters who, first, love the Lord with all their heart and soul. The mistake she made was telling the wrong people. To her surprise, some of her Holy Ghost filled sisters left church and went to her home with the power of a mighty God. The devil knew each one by name. They had a deliverance service and brought her back to church getting back just in time to hear the message—*Pray, Don't Panic.* Now, you tell me if that was not God on the scene? I told you this story to encourage you. Maybe you are there right now. So many families are being affected by the drug business. The good news is **GOD IS MORE THAN ENOUGH!!**

My friend today is still married to that man. He is saved, has been off drugs for years, is filled with the Holy Ghost and living a brand new life. I know when she reads this book that she will know that her life, too, is a living testimony. You do not have to be ashamed to tell others what the Lord has done for you.

> *And they overcame him by the blood of the Lamb, and by the word of their testimony; and they loved not their lives unto the death.*
>
> *Revelation 12:11*

So, let the redeemed of the Lord say so.

Earlier I mentioned that I was suicidal and almost lost my freedom. I literally meant just that. I had been married before, after I graduated from high school. All I could think about was marrying my childhood sweetheart. All through our courtship I remembered his being with other girls. But, why didn't I let him go? **PRIDE!!**

NO PAIN, NO GAIN

I did not grow up around living holy everyday or letting Christ live inside me. I went to Sunday School and church all the time. My oldest sister, Ruthie, made certain of that because my mother was usually working. I knew my sister loved the Lord and was a saint herself, but she never pressed upon me sanctification. Growing up, I witnessed pastors and preachers going in and out of women's houses and motels. You may ask how do I know? I know because I was right in the middle of that mess when I became a young woman.

I actually had older saints telling me that it was okay as long as it was with another Christian. **THE DEVIL IS A LIAR!!!** I never heard anyone across the pulpit say this was wrong. They always said, **"God knows we're only human."** I guess we all were just good old church folks. Today, I know this statement has crippled many believers. It grieves my spirit to know that this is a trick of Satan to keep people in bondage. He keeps laughing at those who still believe that they can live any kind of life and make it into Heaven without a heart transplant and being born again. If you don't read anything else, please stop the devil in his tracks and tell him,

DEVIL, THE BLOOD OF JESUS IS AGAINST YOU AND YOU ARE THE FATHER OF LIES!

Time out, people!! We must stop being PROFESSIONAL CHURCHGOERS. We must stop playing church. Jesus must become the Lord of our lives. We must start right now, living holy. Let me share with you what the Word says:

> *But the cowardly, unbelieving, abominable, murderers, sexually immoral, sorcers, idolaters, and all liars shall have their part in the lake which burns with fire and brimstone, which is the second death.*
> *Revelation 2:1-8*

This is why I am not ashamed to tell young people that sex before marriage is wrong. You might enjoy it for awhile or while you are doing it. But it will COST YOU! SIN COSTS! I fell to that lie at a very young age. As I look back, this, too, was part of God's amazing grace over my life. Whenever I recall my past to help someone in the future a song comes up in my spirit—*He Was There All The Time.*

Young people, if your are thinking about getting married or having sex now, please pray and wait on God. I went into my first marriage totally unequally yoked. I had more problems than any young person should have had to endure. You cannot hold on to someone who does not want you, especially when they are not saved. Also, to the women of today, don't settle for just anyone so you can say you have a man. Tell flesh to **SHUT UP!** Go take a shower, walk around the block, call someone spiritual that can pray you through right now or just stop and holler **HELP!**

NO PAIN, NO GAIN

There was a tragic situation that happened in that marriage. This is when I almost lost all hope for living. I just could not face what I had done to me and my family. I realized too late that this man had never loved me or our child. I was in a hopeless situation. But now!! God's amazing grace, how sweet the sound that saved a wretch like me. I once was lost, but now I am found; was blind but now I see. God's word is true.

> *And we know that all things work together for good to them that love God, to them who are called according to His purpose. For whom he did foreknow, he also did predestinate to be conformed to the image of his Son, that he might be the firstborn among many brethren. Moreover whom he did predestinate, them he also called: and whom he*

God Is More Than Enough

called, them he also justified: and whom
he justified, them he also glorified.
Romans 8:28-30

I must encourage you to keep company with saints somewhere in your life. I remember a coworker, named Emily, that was considered a "Holy Roller." She was, and still is, a wonderful, powerful, praying woman. She got in touch with me and asked if she could pray for me. And I said, "Yes." She did not stop there; she wanted to know if I would allow her pastor to pray for me. What could I say? Where could I go? My life, I thought, had gone to Hell! This was the first time that I really witnessed faith in action, the power of prayer and love. I praise God that I found out there were other people praying for me that I did not know. People were praying all across the country. I will go to my grave believing that the prayers of the saints saved me. I was totally set free---spirit, body, and soul.

My life from that day has never been the same. What happened to me after that? Well, for seven years, I was around the wrong people. All I engaged in were parties, clubs, drinking, and sex. I guess you can say that I was like the *SAMARITAN WOMAN* still looking for love in all the wrong places and had not yet met the man at the well.

During the last part of these seven years there was one friend who got my attention. Her name is Gladys and she was different. I often wondered why she was in the clubs; she seemed so out of place. But, she, too, came from the mindset that *"We're only human."* One thing that caught my attention about Gladys was that she loved going to church and she loved singing. So we started to hang out together doing the church scene. I must say, and she wouldn't mind my saying, that **WE WERE NOT HOLY AT ALL!** But, we did love Jesus. After awhile, I did not feel right doing the things in which we were involved. There was something on the inside happening to me. I wanted more of God and less of men. I was tired of living that half in/half out life. It finally hit me; nothing or no one is worth losing your walk with God and your soul to Hell. If this is where you are---turning to anti-depressants, alcohol, sex, and drugs---this is not the answer.

The answer is **J-E-S-U-S.** Maybe for you that may be hard to believe, but trust me. I trust God in every area of my life. **GOD IS A GOOD GOD! HE IS A GOD THAT IS MORE THAN ENOUGH! PRAISE HIM!**

PERSONAL THOUGHTS

Chapter Two
A TIME, A SEASON, A PURPOSE

*E*verything has its season; there is a time for every purpose under Heaven. (Ecclesiastes 3:1) Why is it so hard for us to accept this? I must stop here to tell you that the enemy is none other than Satan himself. When I found out just how much he hates women, it blew my spiritual mind. Listen to this.

> *And there appeared a great wonder in heaven; a woman clothed with the sun, and the moon under her feet, and upon her head a crown of twelve stars: And she being with child cried, travailing in birth, and pained to be delivered. And there appeared another wonder in*

27

heaven; and behold a great red dragon, having seven heads and ten horns, and seven crowns upon his heads. And his tail drew the third part of the stars of heaven, and did cast them to the earth: and the dragon stood before the woman which was ready to be delivered, for to devour her child as soon as it was born. And she brought forth a man child, who was caught up untoGod, and to his throne. And the woman fled into the wilderness, where she hath a place prepared of God, that they should feed her there a thousand two hundred and threescore days. And there was war in heaven: Michael and his angels fought against the dragon; and the dragon fought and his angels, And prevailed not; neither was their place found any more in heaven. And the great dragon was cast out, that old serpent, called the Devil, and Satan, which deceiveth the whole world: he was cast out into the earth, and his angels were cast out with him. And I heard a loud voice saying in heaven, Now is come salvation, and strength, and the kingdom of our God, and the power of his Christ: for the accuser of our brethren is cast down, which accused them before our God day and night. And they overcame him by the blood of the Lamb, and by the word of their testimony, and they loved not their lives unto the death. Therefore rejoice, ye heavens, and ye that dwell in them. Woe to the inhabiters of the earth and of the sea! For the devil is come down unto you, having great wrath, because he knoweth that he hath but a short time. And when the dragon saw that he was cast unto the earth, he persecuted the woman which brought forth the man child. And to the woman were given two wings of a great eagle, that she might fly into the wilderness, into her place, where she is nourished for a time, from the face of the serpent. And the serpent cast out of his mouth

> *water as a flood after the woman, that he might cause her to be carried away of the flood. And the earth helped the woman, and the earth opened her mouth, and swallowed up the flood which the dragon cast out of his mouth. And the dragon was wroth with the woman, and went to make war with the remnant of her seed, which keep the commandments of God, and have the testimony of Jesus Christ.*
> *Revelation 12:1-17*

If we can stand to be blessed, then maybe God can stand to bless us through our obedience to Jesus. I have learned that judgment is on one side of the coin, and grace and mercy are on the other side. Don't fret about where you are now. Maybe you are not married and getting older day by day. You are not being used in your church. It seems that no one is aware of your giftings; in due season God will open up a door for you. In the book of Isaiah , it reads:

Hast thou not known? hast thou not heard, that the everlasting God, the Lord, the Creator of the ends of the earth, fainteth not, neither is weary? there is no searching of his understanding. He giveth power to the faint; and to them that have no might he increaseth strength. Even the youths shall faint and be weary, and the young men shall utterly fall: But they that wait upon the Lord shall renew their strength; they shall mount up with wings as eagles; they shall run, and not be weary; and they shall walk, and not faint.

Isaiah 40:28-31

A Time, A Season, A Purpose

Please hear me good. You never want a man to give you anything that God has not given to you because if man gives you anything he can take it back in the twinkling of an eye. Even in this season of my life, I still have to humble myself and submit myself to leadership.

I remember after being ordained for about one year, there were many things taking place in my church. I thought I had arrived in Heaven. Oh, I was wrong. Here came another test. My pastor called all of the elders in and announced that only he and his wife would be in charge of all of the duties in the service. Were we hurt? Yes, and I don't think hurt is strong enough to describe the way I felt. I did question God. Did I miss my assignment? Surely he did not send me over here to be persecuted and bound by a man again. What I did not understand then, but I do now is that God was not through with me yet. My acid test with my pastor had not been sealed. And I needed to come **under** some more. So, what did I do? I prayed and cried, prayed and cried. I continued to serve wherever and whenever I was asked. It got to the place where having pulpit duties did not mean much to me anymore. I turned my focus completely on God. The Holy Ghost comforted me and I helped comfort my other friends in the ministry. I received counseling and I shared my counseling with them.

As I close this chapter, don't give up on your dreams. If God said it, stand until His will is clear for your life. You may be going through a test right now in ministry. Just know that God is with you.

NO PAIN!!! NO GAIN!!!

PERSONAL THOUGHTS

_____

_____

_____

_____

_____

_____

_____

_____

_____

Chapter Three
WHEN OTHERS DON'T SEE

*I*n this warfare of victories, you will go from faith to faith, test to test, and glory to glory. Many times during my growth in the Lord, it seemed like I was always running into this spiritual conquest with other saints. Everyone was saved; everybody was filled with the Spirit; everyone read the same word; the Lord spoke to everyone; everyone was strong in what they believed. And with all of that, I stopped one day and asked the Lord, if you really were using one of us, we would miss it! This stirred my spirit.

When Others Don't See

One weekend the word of God poured out so much from my pastor, Destined To Win (DTW) Home Bible Study Group, and an evangelist I had gone to hear, that there was no doubt in my mind that it was Jesus speaking on some of the issues I had faced. Whenever the word comes forth like that, God will hold you accountable for the word you hear.

Faith without works is dead.
James 2:20

Whenever you take the word and put it into action, watch out! All Hell is getting ready to break out in your relationship with others. No one wants familiar friends giving any type of revelation knowledge. People will always say that **I KNEW YOU WHEN!** I must stop and give honor to whom honor is due. There are many great men and women of God who have made an impact on my life including the following: Kenneth & Gloria Copeland, Marilyn Hickey, Benny Hinn, Evangelist Joyce Timmon-Rogers, Myles Munroe, Kenneth Hagin, Prophetess Janice Mixon-Thompkins, Larry Lea, Creflo Dollar, Pastor Gregory Spencer, Fred K.C. Price, Pastor Gene Moore, Oral and Richard Roberts, Dr. Adella Sloan, Joyce Meyer, John Hagee, Dr. James, Bishop T.D. Jakes, and my pastor, Reginald D. Jordan of Inspiring Temple of Praise Church. As you see, over the years, each one had something to do with the changes in my life.

When Others Don't See

You must be willing to give up all to follow Christ—people, places, and things. If you believe in your heart right now that God has given you direction, just do it! But, make sure it is God and not people that have told you it is your time. I stayed at my home church for ten years after knowing in my spirit that God had a call on my life.

I personally did not want to leave my sisters and brothers in the dark any longer as others had left us. If you stay wherever you are now, you must be willing to go through the fire because it will happen. Sometimes I felt that everyone hated me including my husband, mother, and other family members, not to mention my church family where I grew up. I thought that all of these people would have known that God had His hands on me. Many times I had to stand alone on His word. That meant against our pastor, other Sunday School teachers, Mission sisters, sisters in ministry, and many others. Many did not agree with my new found freedom. I started to stand against **WE'RE ONLY HUMAN** theology. I must admit that most of the time I did not deliver the messages correctly because I did not have anyone to teach me what to do with this power that was coming from within me. Many people let me know they did not agree and many would go all around the church to avoid having contact with me. After awhile, I found myself alone.

When Others Don't See

The Holy Ghost had time to reach me and I had time to start listening to his voice. Finally, my pastor saw my heart and knew I just wanted to see people set free and delivered. He gave me his blessings but asked that I never go behind any pulpit because he did not believe in women preaching. I had to honor his wishes. I respected him and I needed to be under his covering to be in order with the Lord.

The Holy Ghost started to teach me how to use wisdom in my walk. Whenever I was invited out, I would let them know right off that I could speak, but not behind the pulpit. After many years, the day finally came for my next level. It was time to move.

NO PAIN, NO GAIN

For a long time I did not know what was going on inside of me. But I did know that the call was getting greater. I started to be very heavy about doing God's will and man's will at the same time. I found out that a choice would have to be made one day.

When that day came, I went to my pastor to let him know that I could not keep my calling a secret any longer. **I AM WHAT I AM BY THE GRACE OF GOD.** God had a work for me to do in His vineyard and the time had come. I knew that I was not going to be disobedient to Him. I praise God that one night I had a chance to talk with the evangelist/pastor that was doing a revival at our church. He counseled me that night on the Word of

God and why men are held bound by traditions. The Word of God says ***Where no counsel is, the people fall: But in the multitude of counselors there is safety.***

But I did not stop with him; I sought other counseling from men of God that I respected in the ministry that understood both my pastor and me. But one thing they told me was that I had to make a choice according to the written Word of God and I must respect my pastor's wishes as long as I was under his leadership. Now I was faced with a hard decision to make. First, because I loved my pastor and my church family where I grew up. But when I put my thoughts on a scale, the Word of God came to my remembrance.

NO PAIN, NO GAIN

We ought to obey God rather than men.
Acts 5:29

I am here to tell you it is impossible to have two masters. I also found out that when people are too familiar with you it is hard for them to respect you as God's vessel. This is just like Aaron and Miriam did Moses.

I remember many times not understanding the actions of my pastor. But, since I have experienced a leadership role, it seems like the Holy Ghost keeps taking me back to people, places, and things. I believe that you can appreciate others after you have traveled in their shoes. It takes time to get it in your head that no other opinion matters except God's.

When Others Don't See

Now, as I am writing at 1:50 AM, the Holy Ghost was saying to me, *"When you missed it, God was still in control of every situation."* Did all this opposition from many whom I loved so dearly make me feel super spiritual or holier than thou (as some would label me)? The answer is NO! Did I try to fight doing what I believe God was telling me to do? The answer is YES! Why? Because I wanted everyone to love PAT and never leave me. My brothers and sisters, Jesus meant exactly what He said in the gospel.

> *He who loves father or mother more than me is not worthy of me. And he that taketh not his cross, and followeth after me, is not worthy of me. He that findeth his life shall lose it: and he that loseth his life for my sake shall find it.*
> *Matthew 10:37-39*

NO PAIN, NO GAIN

When you start living this Word for what it says, **LOOK OUT!!!** You have got a war on your hands. God will tell you where it will come from, so do not be surprised with those who are closer to you. This is not a put down to anyone who may read this and have experienced this with me. It is just the truth. The Word says, *If you know the truth, the truth will make you free. (John 8:32)*

All of my confrontations happened for a reason. Basically, they were for me to grow up and maybe to help someone else. I just had a thought about King Jehoshaphat. The enemy from outside was getting ready to attack the children of God. They all got together for prayer and fasting before God. He heard and answered, *"Do not be afraid nor dismayed because of this great multitude, for the battle is not yours, but God's."* All they needed to do was position themselves, stand still, and see the salvation of the Lord. God is still telling us today to do the same thing today that He told the king—stand and do not worry about others.

Today, we are singing, shouting, praising God, and setting up spiritual ambushes against one another. God will sometimes use the enemy to get our attention and the minute God decides it's time for us to be chastened, the first thing that comes out of our mouth is, **"IT'S THE DEVIL." WAKE UP, SAINTS OF GOD!**

NO PAIN, NO GAIN

My son, do not despise the chastening of the Lord, nor be discouraged when you are rebuked by him; for whom the Lord loves he chastens, and scourges every son whom he receives.

Hebrews 12:5

If you endure chastening, God deals with you as with His sons. For what son is there whom a father does not chasten? No chastening seems to be joyful for the present, but grievous. Nevertheless, afterward, it yields the peaceable fruit of righteousness to those who have been trained by it. We really don't have any problem accepting chastening until it comes from a sister or brother with whom we are familiar. Now we put on our spiritual brakes. Who does she or he think they are? If you would stop and think, maybe God is using them. Maybe they are now the called and chosen of God to help set the captives free and heal the brokenhearted.

I remember one Friday night we attended home bible study. We were studying the book of Romans. This night, the Word was teaching us about *Responsibilities Toward Higher Powers*. If you are a student of God's Word, you are aware that Paul teaches about the functions of human government. But you must remember that God's Word also covers many other areas of governing authorities. Not that I was looking for a word to justify my calling and position, but, I need to know if I was lining up with God's order.

NO PAIN, NO GAIN

I found that in this study, it said, *"For he is God's minister to you for good. But if you do evil, be afraid; for he does not bear the sword in vain, for he is God's minister, an avenger to execute wrath on him who practices evil."* As leaders (those who are leaders), you will find yourself standing naturally alone at times. In this warning, I want to encourage you, if God is with you, who can stand against you? He will bring you through and will confirm that what He was looking for in a person, He found it in you!

I am forty-nine years old now. I was forty-four years old when I started this book. I feel very young at heart, but in my spirit many years have rolled by. Why? I have experienced so many spiritual warfares in the last twenty years of my walk with God. Many nights and days I cried before the Lord. **Why? Why? Why?** If you are young in your calling or ministry, the Bible calls you a novice. We cannot get around suffering for the cause of Christ. If you are suffering, just make sure it is for what you strongly believe. If you are not willing to take a stand, then you will never be used by God. Jesus even said, *"I did not come to bring peace, but sword."* The Word of God is the sword and it is sharp!

When I started to study God's Word and the people He chose, Paul was one with whom I bonded-- the servant of Jesus Christ, called to be an apostle, separated to the Gospel of God. The more I studied Paul and his ministry, the more I wanted to be like him. Was I on a wild goose chase? No! He said that

NO PAIN, NO GAIN

I could follow him as he follows Christ. No, I have not been through beatings, shipwrecks or many of the things Paul suffered, but what I have gone through has been more than enough. I have heard Bishop Jakes say, *"Everybody cannot go through what someone else does because some would lose their minds."* But, praise God, we can take comfort in knowing all things will work for the good of those who love the Lord and who are called according to his purpose.

HALLELUJAH!!

I believe that this chapter alone has already encouraged your heart. You are not alone. I believe that maybe all of us who started out will run into opposition of this kind. The Holy Spirit says to tell you that man, the carnal, will always question your call from God. God told Adam not to eat from the tree. Abel tried to get Cain to understand true offerings. Noah tried to get the people to get ready before the flood came. Abraham tried to get Lot to understand the promise. Jacob could see what Esau did not see about his birth right. Moses tried for over forty years to get the chosen people to understand God. Joseph's brothers had problems understanding his dreams. Deborah tried to get Barak to see his place on the battlefield. Hannah was misunderstood by the man of God, Eli. Samuel tried to get the children of Israel to see that they did not need a king. Saul got mad at David's anointing. Solomon still needed more women. Nehemiah tried to examine rebuilding the wall. Daniel, Shadrach, Meshach, and Abednego tried to explain to the king about their love for God. Don't let me mention Jesus, the most misunderstood of all!

One thing we can rejoice in is that there will come a day when we can see the one who died for us face to face. We can ask Him, Lord, how many times did I miss it? Did you really tell me to do what I thought you told me to do? Did I miss hearing from you? The people I tried to share with, did you divinely direct me to talk with them? So for now, the only thing you and I can do is to keep trusting, praying, and studying His word. If you think you missed God, R-E-P-E-N-T and keep on going!

When Others Don't See

Peter and John were on their journey preaching the gospel (Jesus, the Anointed One, sent from Heaven to destroy your yokes, remove your burdens, and show his powers from on high.) A lame man had just been healed at the Beautiful gate of the temple. What went wrong?

The rulers, elders, and scribes asked them, *"By what power or by what name have you done this?"* After they answered them, they were still not satisfied. Sometimes no matter what you say there are people who won't believe you. But, praise God, there may be someone like Gamaliel, a teacher of the law, held in respect by all the people. He commanded them to leave them alone.

NO PAIN, NO GAIN

Men of Israel, take heed to yourselves what you intend to do regarding these men. For if this plan or this work is of men, it will come of nothing; but if it is of God, you cannot overthrow it, lest you even be found to fight against God.

Acts 5:35,38-39

57

PERSONAL THOUGHTS

Chapter Four
RETREAT TO ADVANCE

I found this very hard to do at first because I am a people person. I like everybody and have always wanted people to like me and to let me hang around them. Here was another lesson for me to learn the hard way.

Jesus gave us such beautiful examples concerning retreating. In reading the gospels, he did this many times and when He would come back, things always happened. He was always different. There was always so much power on Him when He returned. He was actually showing the power of getting away by yourself. Sometimes we need to get away. Separated from all of the voices, I am finding out there are so many benefits in standing still until His will is clear to me.

> *In quietness and in confidence shall be*
> *your strength.*
> *Isaiah 30:15*

Quietness is a place where great ideas can be birthed. There are times when we should not talk on the phone, visit or go out, times when there should be no one but you and God. The next thing we need to have is a place of refuge, whether it is in the bathroom, study, living room, closet, kitchen, or driving in your car. All of my healings came when I retreated and went before God.

When it seemed like everybody had turned their backs on me, I found so much comfort in God's word. This scripture is one of my favorites.

Be of good courage, in you O Lord, I put my trust; let me never be ashamed; deliver me in your righteousness. Bow down your ear to me, deliver me speedily, be my rock of refuge, a fortress of defense to save me. For you are my rock and my fortress; therefore, for your name sake, lead me and guide me, for you are my strength. Into your hand I commit my spirit; you have redeemed me, O Lord God to truth. I am a reproach (blame) among all my enemies, but especially among my

> *neighbors (those in the household of faith), and am repulsive to my acquaintances; those who see me outside flee from me. I am forgotten like a dead man, out of mind; I am like a broken vessel. But as for me, I trust in you, O Lord; my times are in your hand; make your face shine upon your servant; do not let me be ashamed, O Lord, for I have called upon you; let the lying lips be put to silence, which speak insolent (insulting) things proudly and contemptuously against the righteous.*

> *Psalm 31*

Some people will tell you that it is wrong to speak in this manner, but that is not true. Paul, himself, said on many occasions that *"I do not boast in myself, but I do boast in the Lord."* You must know who you are, what you have in Jesus, where you stand with Jesus, and what you can do in Jesus. Amen.

Can you feel his presence right now? Can you feel your insides turning? I can hardly type because God is doing a new thing in my life right now. I had no idea that a book was inside of me, but praise God this is just another way I can be a witness while I am here on Earth. This is also something I can leave with you when I have gone home to be with my Lord and Savior, Jesus.

PERSONAL THOUGHTS

_____

_____

_____

_____

_____

_____

_____

_____

_____

_____

_____

_____

Chapter Five
CAN WE WALK TOGETHER?

*I*n 1987, I became very hungry for spiritual food. I was going to church very faithfully, taught Sunday School, and was an usher. I was in a Mission Women's group, but something was still missing in my spiritual walk with God. I believed I was saved. I was raised in a traditional Baptist church and was taught to believe in "Once Saved, Always Saved." People often said that there was one thing that was true about Baptists. We could save someone through the ROMANS ROAD, but could not show them how to live holy.

Can We Walk Together?

I actually knew people who would tell me that the life that the apostles lived, that the prophets lived, and that Jesus lived, was not one that we could live. We could not be that holy. When I became a born again Christian, my spirit could not receive that any longer.

LIVING HOLY IS STILL RIGHT AND LIVING IN THE FLESH IS STILL WRONG!

For those of you who do not know me, personally, you should be able to see by what you have read that I have taken off on a spiritual race against this teaching of "Once Saved, Always Saved." Did all Hell break out when I spoke against this? YES! But I was determined that God had saved me for a purpose and there must be a change in me. You may be in this same situation right now. This is not

NO PAIN, NO GAIN

meant to put down my pastor at that time or my church. They taught what they had been taught. I still love them very much. You may ask me why? I observed many people leaving our church when I was a young woman. Then one day, I realized that those that had left the church were coming into a greater light and those of us left behind were still wandering in the wilderness. No one wanted to endure the hardship as a good soldier. It seemed as if no one wanted to fight the good fight of faith. So what did I do? I started to venture outside of the four walls of our traditional settings and found that there was a world of spirituality that we had not yet touched.

Can We Walk Together?

I wanted to help others to grow, but I discovered that this was not easy. People DO NOT like change! My own husband, mother, and other relatives, also, did not like change. In fact, they all thought that I was going crazy. However, I must stop and give God praise for one that did believe the report. Her name is Linda and she is now a friend, prayer partner, and co-laborer in the ministry.

When I was near a very low point in this flight, I started to feel like Elijah (I Kings 19:1-18). It was then that God connected me with her. We had been together in the ministry for more than fifteen years. Was the relationship tested? YES! Every relationship will go through a test. Paul, Barnabas, John Mark,

NO PAIN, NO GAIN

Peter and Jesus—all went through a relationship check.

Now, it is time to focus on what will unify us as Christians, not what divides us as saints. My pastor preached one Sunday morning—"It's Okay to Be Different As Long As It Is For God." How many brothers and sisters all over this land would be united if we would renew our minds like Christ Jesus.

I have already shared with you the history of Satan and the women in an earlier chapter. I can boldly say, **I AM A WOMAN! I AM A SAVED WOMAN! I AM A WIFE! I AM A MOTHER! I AM A SERVANT! I AM A TEACHER OF THE GOSPEL AND I AM A PREACHER!**

Can We Walk Together?

Oh, wait just one minute. I have gone too far now. A preacher? YES! They said that God does not call women into this area. The problem I had with this, as a Christian young woman, is that it was acceptable for preachers to sleep with us at conventions, but it was not acceptable for us to leave that RAT RACE and PREACH for Jesus. It is so strange to me that this same gender (WOMEN) taught 95% of the preachers (MEN) today to preach the Good News—their mothers. I believe that if it had not been for saved mothers and grandmothers, there would not be any sons in the ministry today.

When God arrested my spirit, I was laying in the hospital waiting to have emergency surgery in 1987. He gave me a vision about my future. I knew what I heard and understood that it was going to get me in serious trouble with my pastor. God did not let my present state of mind interfere with His discussion about my calling. He made it plain to me that it was not my battle and that I should not fight against my pastor or try to change his mind about his belief. If He took care of Pharaoh for Moses and the children of Israel, He would take care of all of my oppositions. Here I stood like another Moses. I praise God that He did not leave me ignorant because the Holy Spirit was there to give me direction.

Compelled to get more knowledge in the Word of God, after going to the Rhema Conference in 1988, I decided to enroll in a correspondence Bible school under the leadership of Kenneth Hagin Ministries of

Can We Walk Together?

Oklahoma. It took me seven years to complete the home study. Through this study, I learned discipline, steadfastness, and to never give up. It was a great challenge for me because I still had to work, be a wife and mother, and be faithful to my church duties. But, praise God anyhow! I got my beautiful diploma in January, 1998. Allow me to share this prophecy found in the book of Acts 2:16-21.

> *But this is that which was spoken by the prophet Joel; And it shall come to pass in the last days, saith God, I will pour out of my Spirit upon all flesh: and your sons and your daughters shall prophesy, and your young men shall see visions, and your old men shall dream dreams: And on my servants and on my handmaidens I will pour out in those days of my Spirit; and they shall prophesy: And I will shew wonders in*

> *heaven above, and signs in the earth beneath; blood, and fire, and vapour of smoke: The sun shall be turned into darkness, and the moon into blood, before that great and notable day of the Lord come: And it shall come to pass, that whosoever shall call on the name of the Lord shall be saved.*

Always remember that the devil's job is to keep God's people divided over issues like this. Please hear me. God does not want us trying to prove our calling to anyone. We really don't have time for that. Just let the Word of God speak for itself. The battle is the Lord's! The victory is ours! Remember His Word:

> *Moreover whom he did predestinate, them he also called: and whom he called, them he also justified: and*

73

> ***whom he justified, them he also
> glorified. What shall we then say to
> these things? If God be for us, who can
> be against us?***
> ***Romans 8:30-31***

Saints of God, don't you see it yet! It is all about Jesus; it is not about us. Men and women of God, it is not about titles; it is not about being called Doc, Rev, or Minister. It is about Jesus!! It is not about where you stand or where you sit; it is about Jesus! What are we really looking for in this ministry walk? Are we seeking man's applause or God's approval? I ask you now can we walk together as children of God, children that are born again by the blood of Jesus Christ, our Lord and Savior? The Bible tells us that there is one God, one faith, and one baptism. Is this enough for us to agree as touching?

PERSONAL THOUGHTS

Chapter Six
THEY OVERCAME BY THE BLOOD

*A*re you ready? I know that I am. It is time. I am so tired of seeing saints fight one another. How can we walk together except we agree? How can we tell others the wages of sin is death, but the gift of God is eternal life? Are we ready to be a true witness of the cross? We don't have to die for anyone. Jesus has already paid the price.

Sometimes when I reread the Old Testament, I think of the many little animals that were sacrificed at the altar and died for people who still could not live holy. Talk about animal rights! Animals may not have had souls, but they felt pain and bled just like you and me. But God allowed it to take place. Why? Because we were the only creation that was created in His image and His likeness.

Let's start today focusing on the blood. I have been told that Jesus' blood did it once and for all! It is not as hard as it seems. I heard a message from Tim Storey—*Just Stretch Out Your Hand of Faith.* What does that mean? It means we must trust God to handle any situation deep down inside of us. Aren't you thankful that Jesus paid the price?

One night at our home Bible study, the Spirit of the Lord was speaking. I was talking about what Jesus had done and how he hung on the cross. In the middle of my flowing with the Spirit, the Holy Ghost stopped me at the part of the story when the sky turns black. In the many sermons I had heard, they said that it was about three hours that the sun refused to shine. The Holy Ghost said, "Can you just imagine in your mind that it was the sins of the whole world? I shared it with the group. We just stopped for a moment and thanked God.

There is no sin in my life that he has not taken care of. The devil would like for us to think that you have really messed up this time. But, you only need to repent. **GOD IS TIME! HE CAN ADJUST TIME TO GIVE YOU HIS MERCY TO STRAIGHTEN UP!**

They Overcame By The Blood

There have been times when standing as a leader I just did not know how, when, and where God was going to fix the problem. I just had to believe that he would do it in His own timing. I praise Him that He is in control and that I am not.

There is another thought about His blood—The Lord's Supper. In thinking about food, you realize that you cannot eat again until your body has done something with what you have already eaten. Praise God! He is waiting on us to finish eating what we think will satisfy us, but there is one meal that many of us have not eaten. He said, *"Take, eat, this is my body which is broken for you; do this in remembrance of me."* What should we remember? We should remember that it was Jesus who paid the price. It is Jesus that keeps interceding for us when we miss it. Nobody but Jesus! After the same manner, also he took the cup, when he had supped, saying, *"This cup is the new testament in my blood: this do ye, as oft as ye drink it, in remembrance of me. (I Corinthians 11:25)*

We have so much to be thankful for. It is all in the blood. What can wash away my sins? Nothing, but the blood of Jesus. What can make me whole again? Nothing, but the blood of Jesus. So let a man examine himself, before he eats of that bread and drinks of that cup. Don't play games with yourself! Your are the one wasting your time. It is time to be honest with yourself. Get completely honest. The choice is yours.

God allows us to dig our own holes; He lets us examine ourselves and He is so kind and true. Even though we blame Him for our downfalls, it is not His fault. He said, *"for this reason many are weak and sickly among you and many sleep."* *(I Corinthians 11:30)* People, let's stop sleepwalking. Wake Up! Judgment Day is coming! If we don't come to ourselves, some of us will die the second death. I cannot emphasize enough that this walk should be about Jesus. I know that blood is rich in its color; I also know that Jesus is rich in all of His promises to man.

PERSONAL THOUGHTS

Chapter Seven
HALLELUJAH, ANYHOW!

*T*his title includes two of the most comforting words that I enjoy sharing with the hurting, confused, and disgusted servants of God---**HALLELUJAH, ANYHOW!** This phrase is so strong for a witness because, as servants of the highest God, we will suffer in this life. Sometimes this life can be very unfair. I cannot begin to tell you how many situations and circumstances I have fallen into that taught me how to encourage myself. Many times I learned this through tears streaming down my face and my heart beating very rapidly inside. Oh! How I wished that someone could have just stopped by and taken the pain away. I must tell you that it is not that easy. Sometimes the pain and tears may last for hours, days, or nights. But I do know that Jesus will never leave you comfortless just like He promised. There is an art to praising God. I guarantee you the more you press through with praises, the better you will feel. How can we feel good with all these bills due and no money? The only way to do this is to stand on the Word of God. But, you must take the time out to find the word you need to stand on to praise God.

Let's look at praises for finances. These are the facts: You have no money at all and the creditors are calling. What must you do? Praise God anyhow! Talk to yourself with the Word.

NO PAIN, NO GAIN

Therefore I (Jesus) say to you, Do not worry about your life, what you will eat or what you will drink; nor about your body, what you will put on. Is not your life more than food and the body more than clothing? Look at the birds of the air, for they neither sow nor reap, nor gather into barns; yet your Heavenly Father feeds them. Are you not more valuable than they? Which of you by worrying can add one cubit to his stature? So why do you worry about clothing? Consider the lilies of the field, how they grow: they neither toil nor spin; and yet I say to you that Even Solomon in all his glory was not arrayed like one of these. Now if God so clothes the grass of the field, which today is, and tomorrow is thrown into the oven, will He not much more clothe you, o you of little faith? Therefore do not worry, saying, What shall we eat? or, What shall we drink? or, What shall we

> *wear? For after all these things the Gentiles seek. For your Heavenly Father knows that you need all these things. But seek first the kingdom of God and His righteousness, and all these things shall be added to you. Therefore do not worry about tomorrow; for tomorrow will worry about its own things. Sufficient for the day is its own trouble.*
> *Matthew 6:23-34*

Don't you feel a praise coming on? Just stop right now and begin to give God the thanks for what He is doing now!!! Ask Him to give you the serenity to accept the things you cannot change and the courage to change the things you can, but the wisdom to know the difference. Amen.

NO PAIN, NO GAIN

Just today, as we made home visits, the spirit of praise came forth through those who had received some type of deliverance through the laying on of hands. How? How can anyone praise God when their body is racking with pain? How can anyone praise God when their body has become disfigured? How can anyone praise God when the doctor has said, "You only have a few months to live." How, how, how? You must be crazy! Well, I am! I am crazy enough to believe everything God has said through the Logos word (spoken word) will come to pass.

The problem with many who are facing such situations is that they do not know what God's word has said. Know the truth and the truth shall make you free. We think that the Bible says the truth will SET you free. That is not what the Word says in John 8:32. It reads, ***And ye shall know the truth, and the truth shall make you free.*** We must search the scriptures.

> ***Who has believed our report? And to whom has the arm of the Lord been revealed? For he shall grow up before him as a tender plant, and as a root out of dry ground. He has no form or comeliness: And when we see him, there is no beauty that we should desire him. He is despised and rejected by men, a man of sorrows and acquainted with grief. And we hid, as it were, our faces from him: He was despised and we did not esteem him. Surely he has borne our griefs and carried our sorrows; yet we esteemed him stricken, smitten by God, and afflicted. But he was wounded for our transgressions, he was bruised for our iniquities; the***

NO PAIN, NO GAIN

> *chastisement for our peace was upon*
> *him, and by his stripes we are healed.*
> *Isaiah 53:1-5*

Hallelujah! Praise God! Don't you see now just what Jesus has done? Maybe, that is still not enough for you. If you still have not received your breakthrough, let's look at some more of the Word.

> *And when he had called his twelve*
> *disciples to him, he gave them power*
> *over unclean spirits, to cast them out,*
> *and to heal all kinds of disease.*
> *Matthew 10:1*

HALLELUJAH!

Hallelujah, Anyhow!

Nothing is too hard for God. He is God, the only God, who is more than enough! Jesus is still much alive today! He has not changed. He has not turned His back on us. But, children of the most High God, we must give Him the praise anyhow. Whatever day it is in your life, this is the day that the Lord has made. Choose to rejoice and be glad about it. This statement is not just a song we sing. It is based on the Word of God. Don't wait until Sunday morning comes.

We have covered financial praise and healing praise. What do we see in our marriage? Do we see hope to cope? Or faith to make it? Let me tell you that it is not easy following the Word of God concerning marriage when you know that things are not what they should be. The Bible tells us not to depart from our husband. So the question is how long Lord do we wait for a change to come? Yes, many husbands or wives want to stay with a godly person and many make their lives a living Hell day by day, week after week, minute by minute. Our only comfort of hope is that our lifestyle one day will sanctify that man or woman. We do have some help. If that unbeliever wants to hit the door; open it. You have just received your breakthrough.

I believe that God still honors marriage and He will give you the grace that is needed to endure. The enemy will only come against those who are a threat to his kingdom. I was a part of a conference in Beaumont, TX—*Resurrection Power for Dead Situations*. There is no situation in your marriage that you cannot give to God. This is a good time to face the facts. Maybe he or she still comes home late, still runs around, still drinks, still doesn't have any money, won't go to church, won't pay tithes or bills, and won't go to counseling. Well, hallelujah, anyhow! Praise your way through to your victory!

PERSONAL THOUGHTS

_____

_____

_____

_____

_____

_____

_____

_____

_____

_____

_____

Chapter Eight
DYING TO SELF

*S*elf is the most dangerous part of God's creation. Self wants so much for so little. There must come a time in our lives that we, as children of God and people of His creation, realize that self can destroy us. I am starting to realize that by focusing on self, I have opened the door to so many attacks. My mind was always trying to do what **I** thought God was telling me to do. When, in actuality, it was self. I believe that I can help somebody by being very honest. It is not wrong to want to please God in our actions, but it is a shame if, what we are doing is for self-glorification.

Dying To Self

I remember deceiving myself by thinking that if people would look at where I came from, where I am now, and where I am headed, they would know that God's glory is on me. Well, let me tell you that God doesn't need our help to show His glory. I was fooled into thinking that He did. I had to learn how to rest in the Lord.

> *Fret not...trust in the Lord...Delight yourself in the Lord...Commit your way unto the Lord...Rest in the Lord and wait patiently for him...Cease from anger, and forsake wrath.*
> *(Psalm 37:1-8)*

All of what David said will take the pressure off of our having to make ourselves better. Can't you see now that we are nothing without the power of the anointing of God in us? **HALLELUJAH!** I want to encourage you that all is well as long as we try not to fix things.   I was blessed to attend a Leadership Conference with Dr. Myles Munroe. I can tell you once again that my eyes were illuminated. If we are serious about wanting to walk in the perfect will of God, we must first be honest with ourselves.

> *And you have forgotten the exhortation which speaks to chastening of the Lord, nor be discouraged when you are rebuked by him; for whom the Lord loves he chastens, and scourges every son who he receives. If you endure chastening, God deals with you as with sons (male or females). Now no*

> *chastening seems to be joyful for the present, but grievous; nevertheless, afterward it yields the peaceable fruit of righteousness to those who have been trained by it.*
>
> *Hebrews 12:5-11*

Self always hates to admit I missed it. But if the Holy Ghost is living inside of you it is not hard. All we have to do is to remind self what the Word says. We can rejoice (jump up, move, shout!!!) and say that God sees our heart and knows the intent of our mind. If we miss it, REPENT! I have learned that when you see "RE-", it means returning back to its original state.

NO PAIN, NO GAIN

As time passes in our lives, it will become less important what people think, how people think you should be, or where people think you should go. I have made a renewed commitment to God—His way or no way!

Take a moment to reflect back on why, where, when, what, and how God spoke to your heart. Be proud that you are dying daily in your flesh. Say with me these words—*It is not I that liveth, but the Christ who lives inside of me.*

PERSONAL THOUGHTS

_____

_____

_____

_____

_____

_____

_____

_____

_____

Chapter Nine
HOW TO SURVIVE THE THERMOSTAT MAN

*Y*ou may be wondering how did I ever come up with this title. Well, one thing that I have experienced in this Christian walk is that you will encounter people who believe that they have special callings and anointings on their lives to monitor how you should act, speak, and believe. I believe that they think that they are on a divine assignment.

It has taken me awhile to realize what happened to me after coming in contact with such a person. At first I thought it was such a blessing to have someone that wanted what God had given me. But after awhile the nightmare began. Many times I wanted that person completely out of sight and out of mind. But I kept hearing God say, *"My grace is sufficient."* This person wanted to analyze everything, everybody, every word, every move, every speaker, every preacher, and the list goes on and on. This person's ways caused many conflicts, disagreements, and unrest. I hope you are getting the picture because just in case the person reads this book, I do not want to start all over again explaining why I wrote this.

Let me take a moment to explain the spiritual thermostat. That is when someone is on your trail keeping a scorecard. Their scale will tell them when you are powerful, anointed, wise, full of wisdom, in self, or angry. Have you ever experienced meeting someone like this? You may be reading this book and say to yourself, Yes, when you first met me. Yes, at one time I was this person. I thank God that He is rearranging me and has changed me.

Many times, because of zeal in our early stages of progression, we will error. We spend lots of precious moments measuring other Christians' walk. God has already given us His spiritual thermostat; you will find it in Matthew 12:33—*Either make the tree good and its fruit good; or make the tree bad and its fruit bad: for a tree is known by its fruit.*

How to Survive the Thermostat Man

I plead with the saints of God, pastors, fivefold ministers, and critics—lets get our eyes off the thermostat and do the work that God has called each one of us to do. I believe that God is tired of the warfare that is happening between His children. I decided that it was time for me to be free from the bondage of man.

I was raised in a traditional Baptist church and was faithful to my church and pastor. However, as the level of the Word increased in my heart, I could not contain the Word anymore; it was time to walk. This particular denomination did not accept women preachers. I want to inform my readers that denominational walls are coming down, just like God brought the Berlin Wall down! Getting free is not easy. It will take praying, fasting, and being around stronger believers.

Maybe I have found your heartbeat. You are in a church that is not going anywhere and doesn't want you to go anywhere. You must seek the Lord while He may be found. Call on Him while He is near. Who is gauging you? Who has the right to gauge your anointing? Has God really appointed your scorekeeper?

Just a footnote to leave with those who are in the ministry. There is one person who has the right to keep scores on you and that is your Pastor or Overseer. I do believe that it is necessary to have someone to help guide you in the right direction. Many churches today would not be led by incompetent pastors if someone had taken the time to say wait, slow down, pray first.

PERSONAL THOUGHTS

Chapter Ten
BE FOUND GUILTY

*Y*ou are now summoned to appear before the

JUDGMENT SEAT OF CHRIST, held in Courtroom

Heaven, following the rapture of the Church.

On the ___, day in the year of _____, Bro.

Whosoever & Sis. Whosoever were found praising

God with their hands lifted high saying that:

> *I will extol you, O Lord, for you have*
> *lifted me up and have not let my foes*
> *rejoice over me. O Lord my God, I cried*
> *out to you, and you have healed me. O*
> *Lord, you have brought my soul up*
> *from the grave; you have kept me alive*
> *that I should not go down to the pits of*

> *Hell. Sing praises to the Lord, you saints of his, and give thanks at the remembrance of his holy name. For his anger is but for a moment; his favor is for life: weeping may endure for a night, but joy comes in the morning. (Psalm 30:1-5)*

On the ___, day in the year of _____, Bro. Whosoever & Sis. Whosoever were found loving their enemies, blessing those who cursed them, doing good to those who hated them, and praying for those who spitefully used them and persecuted them. They were telling people that the Word of God said:

> *For if you love those who love you, what reward have you? (Matthew 5:46)*

NO PAIN, NO GAIN

On the ___, day in the year of _____, Bro. Whosoever & Sis. Whosoever were found giving their last away. Saying, *Give and it shall be given to you: good measure, pressed down, shaken together, and running over will be put into your bosom. For with the same measure that you use, it will be measured back to you again. (Luke 6:38)*

On the ___, day in the year of _____, Bro. Whosoever & Sis. Whosoever were found forgiving 70 x 7 times when the same people continued to treat them like dogs. They believed that *for the one who had an unbelieving spouse that if he is willing to live with her, let her not divorce him and if a husband has a wife who does not believe, if she is willing to live with him, let him not divorce her. Saying they can be sanctified through them. (I Corinthians 7:13-16)*

On the ___, day in the year of _____, Bro. Whosoever & Sis. Whosoever were found *studying to show themselves approved unto God, a workman that need not to be ashamed, rightly dividing the word of truth. (II Timothy 2:15)*

So, Judge, we rest our case!

NO PAIN, NO GAIN

JUDGE: You have heard the charges brought against you. How do you plead? Guilty or not guilty?

YOU: GUILTY!

JUDGE: I THEN SENTENCE YOU TO ETERNAL LIFE!!!

CASE CLOSED!

PERSONAL THOUGHTS

_____

_____

_____

_____

_____

_____

_____

_____

_____

_____

_____

Chapter Eleven
THE MYSTERY OF THE UNKNOWN CONDUCTOR

*B*ack in the summer of 1996, I thought this book was finally coming to a close. I had selected a publisher, received a quote, and was waiting for the money to come. The money did not come in fast enough so the publisher sent my master copy back to me. I did not lose hope because where God guides, He will provide!

One day I was visiting one of my sisters in Christ and her sister, Shirley, stopped by. Shirley became a personal intercessor for this book. She, has always, asked how the book was coming. After giving her the report, another prophecy came from her mouth—***The book is not finished yet.*** That stayed with me throughout the night because if the book was not finished, then that meant more suffering was on the way. At that time, I thought I had experienced the deepest pain that anyone on this Earth could have experienced in Jesus. Oh! But was I so wrong. My next test was on its way. My sister Hattie's life was coming to an end on this Earth. The holidays were here and Hattie had the family over to her house for Thanksgiving dinner. Hattie loved to cook and I did not. Something was very strange this time. Hattie was struggling to enjoy herself. She did not look good at all, so I suggested that we eat and leave so Hattie could go to bed. The next day, my mother informed me that her husband had to take her to the hospital that night. They put her in ICU. I could not go to see her right away because I was ill myself. I did not want her to catch my cold. Well, I finally got a chance to visit her and the report was good. She was finally transferred to a room.

The following Saturday I took my mother to a funeral and told her I would take her to the hospital to see Hattie. My mother and I stopped to eat first and stayed in the car for about ten minutes to eat. At the hospital, we entered the doors, walked down the corridors, and rode up the elevator to the second floor. The doors opened and we went to the right. There I could see Hattie sitting upright in the bed. The closer

I got to her I knew something was wrong. She did not recognize that we were approaching her. Because of the quickening of the Holy Spirit, I wheeled my mother back out as quickly as I could. I then walked to Hattie, went to her chest, and commanded her to live and not die in the name of Jesus! At that time, the nurse heard me and called CODE BLUE.

I continued to do warfare. I called all the prayer warriors' telephone numbers that I could remember. I told them to sound the alarm; the enemy was trying to steal, kill and destroy Hattie. The doctor came out to tell us that her brain had been without oxygen too long and there was nothing else they could do. By this time, I was ready for war!!!

NO PAIN, NO GAIN

Now here came a test like never before. I prayed and cried, prayed and cried, but nothing was changing in the natural. What went wrong? Why didn't my prayers and others' prayers turn this situation around? Who was orchestrating this event that was hurting so bad? Finally, the Holy Ghost spoke to my heart. Do you remember the story of Shadrach, Meshach, and Abednego in the fiery furnace with Nebuchadnezzar. I said Yes. So now is the time for you to take a stand in your spirit.

> *My God whom I serve is able to deliver, but if not, let it be known that he is still God. (Daniel 3:17-18)*

The Mystery of the Unknown Conductor

No one was allowed in her presence that did not have faith. After seven days on the life support machine, the doctor told us we had to make a decision about what the family would do. We all gathered around her bed and talked to her and God. We trusted Him to make the right decision for her future. So, He, being the God that He is, would not have her to stay here without being whole.

I have shared this chapter with you because many Christians do not want to accept God's ways sometimes. Yes, He is a healer. Yes, He is a prayer hearing God, but everything in life has a season *To everything there is a season, a time for every purpose under Heaven: a time to be born, and a time to die. (Ecclesiastes 3:1)*

NO PAIN, NO GAIN

The master has told us that *we shall not all sleep, but we shall be changed in a moment, in the twinkling of an eye. The trumpet will sound, and the dead will be raised first and we who are alive will be changed. Don't be ignorant, brethren concerning those who have fallen asleep, lest you sorrow as others who have no hope. (I Thessalonians 4:9-18)*

To every reader who has taken the time to purchase and read about my struggles in this life, may you be encouraged by my life to press on toward the mark of the higher calling for your life.

I know that this is not the end of the story. Before this book is published, there is one more pain I must add to my chapter of life. That is my dear mother, Ruth A. Perkins. She went home to be with the Lord on February 21, 2000.

NO PAIN, NO GAIN!!!

PERSONAL THOUGHTS

_____

_____

_____

_____

_____

_____

_____

_____

_____

PERSONAL THOUGHTS

_____

_____

_____

_____

_____

_____

_____

_____

_____

_____

The Teaching Ministry of Elder Pat Miller

Audio Cassette Series

Come Ye To The Water	2 tapes	$10.00
The Hidden Face of God	2 tapes	$10.00
Get Ready! Set! Go!	2 tapes	$10.00

Single Audio Cassette

If I Have to Fight You, I'll Fight You On My Knees	$ 5.00
Be Careful How You Live!	$5.00

To contact Pat Miller for speaking engagements, or to order cassette tapes or books, write or call:

Inspiring Temple of Praise Church
2012 E. Lancaster Ave.
Fort Worth, TX 76103
ATTN: Elder Pat Miller
(817) 870-9828   Telephone
(817) 870-9855   Fax